As A Man Is

Man Is

Quotable Poems and Lyrics

Credits

Several of the poems in this volume previously appeared in the following publications:

The Georgia Cracker Magazine
The Think Tank
Westminster Magazine
Wesleyan Christian Advocate
Friends Magazine
(The Original) Athens Magazine
The Live Wire
Science of Mind Magazine
The Span Magazine
"Different" Magazine
Reflections Magazine
The Pow-Wow Magazine

As A Man Is

Quotable Poems and Lyrics

Frank Harmon, Jr.

Pentland Press, Inc.
England • USA • Scotland

Published By Pentland Press, Inc.
5124 Bur Oak Circle, Raleigh, North Carolina 27612
United States of America
919-782-0281
ISBN 1-57197-070-3

Library of Congress Catalog Card Number 97-65970
Copyright © 1997 Frank Harmon, Jr.

Printed in the United States of America

To my mother,
Glennice Olive LeFurgey Harmon;
poet, writer and musical prodigy who was a great
inspiration in my life.

"As a man is, so he sees."

Frank Harmon, Jr., "Cherokee Phoenix"
yearbook, 1949, Reinhardt College

The poems and lyrics in this volume were written while the author was a student at the University of Georgia and Reinhardt College and while residing in Atlanta and Athens, Georgia. They span a period from 1947 into 1996.

I.

O Words That Will Not Let Me Go

Bouquets

I bring bouquets of words,
And if the blooms aren't living,
I hope you'll feel as I do,
That the gift is in the giving.

Incapability

I cannot say the things that I desire to,
Save on this paper—for my spoken word
Sounds hollowly, when I wish to set fire to
The thoughts my drinking eyes may gird.

Then will you grant me a look of understanding,
As if the words—I had already said them?
Forgive my blunders—how you feel notwithstanding;
For when they're said I can't help where I've led them.

Voices at Midnight

The cynic in me says,

"There are no new trails of thought—

Each thought a hand-me-down,

Each inspiration from a used bargain sale."

But the optimist replies, "Pioneer! Arise

From your mental sleep. Open

The mind's eye, free the mind's ear.

New trails await you. You can be

The Columbus poet.

Pioneer!"

Two voices calling.

Which shall I heed?

Time will tell . . .

Walt Whitman

I with my pebbles in song,
musically tossed, yet remembering,
I have need of your hands, Walt,
sturdy and sure, guiding me
in my tossing, choosing
my objectives, breaching the gap
between man and man.
Here, Walt, here beside me,
hand in hand, old friend,
you guiding, I quickstepping
by your side. Come with me,
Walt. I have need of you.
America has need of you.
Will you not come?

To The Scoffers

"He speaks a false language," they say . . .

But I say my speech is clear and single,

for I talk of common things.

    And I sing of Earth's children

    and Earth's scars,

    and life's long-drawn question,

for these are the things I see,

and the things I hear,

and the things I feel . . .

Vers

The poet writes poems
about poetry and poets;
and so,
a poet is a poet
in a poet's eyes.

The Non-Poet

He lives all day on poetry and dreams
washing down
his bit of food each meal
and yet he hungers
and yet his brain and heart
each craves
a thousand more poetry days . . .
but he would not admit it
he would not own up
to liking it
he would scorn good music
and laugh guiltily
at a poem
or poets . . .

I Am a Thousand Voices

I am a thousand voices,
singing a thousand songs,
one of them being:
Give me a life that is one long kiss,
a loving of love.
Love asks nothing, needs nothing,
wants nothing more than this . . .
   and why should I—
   and why should I?

The Whisperer

The Whisperer . . .

He sings new words to old tunes

while dreamy eyes shut themselves

and willing ears listen to his songs . . .

Have you heard this deep music?

Have you seen rememberings

dancing in the fire?

It was only the Whisperer . . .

Only the Whisperer

You saw . . .

You heard . . .

The Greater Question

Life
is a vagueness;
a searching
for clarity;
a probing
into the unknown;
a struggling
with a never-tamed frontier.

We come
knowing nothing;
we leave
wondering much.

I Know Nothing

I know that I know nothing.

Nothing

may be a fine thing to know.

The world . . .

this life . . .

myself . . .

all may be nothing.

And if they be,

I pride myself.

I am well-versed . . .

I know nothing.

Nothings

The world

Is a handful of nothings.

And I—

I am one of those nothings.

You certainly

Have to work hard

In this old world

For the privilege of being

A

Nothing.

On and On

Wandering, groping blindly

in a hall of mirrors,

seeking myself,

listening

for a half-remembered

   voice,

reaching out

to a half-remembered

   face,

yet still

my identity remains unknown,

and I have never met

myself.

Identity

I was not me, yesterday—
I must have been
that strange creature
who lived before the last death
and reincarnation—
for that was not me.

No, not mine,
those strange thoughts
and stranger yearnings,
though I shall not disown them—
they were above me;
I had to reach loftily
to touch them with
my fingertips . . .

I was not me, yesterday—
I was someone else,
or a dark mixture
of several used-to-beings . . .

Mr. Nobody Wonders

Sometimes
I wonder what would happen if
the world were to stop running blindly
into the same old blue haze
and God were to sit down on His one-spot
all day long and do nothing
but munch peanuts and read the funny papers
all day long
all day long
nothing happening, not one single solitary
event to scribble down
for some future fool to memorize . . .

But
the world's gotta keep on running
into the everlasting blue haze
so the Lord won't sit around
all day munching peanuts
and reading the funny papers . . .

Time and Space

I am the measureless sky,
Nether region of life-span.
I am the toilsome steps
To nowhere and everywhere
And the countless millions
Who tread their lives away
Upon them.

Nameless

I've got that feeling
again.
Don't know what it is.
It remains
nameless.
Some folks might scoff
and say
I've never had it at all.
I know differently.
I've felt it
surging within me,
clutching at my very being.

Yet
all the while
the feeling and I
are strangers
together
in a foreign land,
and we clasp hands

brother-like,
not knowing
each other's names
but friends
just the same,
working together
toward a common
goal—
it, too,
vague,
nameless.

Today

Today
is a one-way street
that leads
to tomorrow.

Encounter

Tomorrow is over the tree line,

And yesterday's under my feet;

And somewhere between the dark and the seen,

Today is the day that I meet.

Total

Life,
Algebraic—
Mostly
The unknown factors.

Small beginnings,
Acorn to oak.
Small endings,
Dust to God.

Taps, Taps, Taps

Taps, taps, taps:
Taps for you, for me,
as the earth's doors close,
Taps for everyone . . .

Yes, taps for everyone—taps for you,
for me; dearth-notes for the masses,
the kings, alike, Gabriel's golden trumpet
(the one that men have said
will one day sound—one day? why, it
has sounded for millions of years,
since the advent of man, for every man,
it sounds, hear its sweet echo?)
will someday sound for all of us—
there is no injustice in heaven,
each of us shall get his due, his taps.

Taps, taps, taps,
Taps for you, for me,
as the earth's doors close,
Taps for everyone . . .

Night

Night is the closest akin to Death,
And yet it has its sweet repose . . .
Night is only the Garden of Death,
Where the everlasting darkness grows.

Mystery

Death is deathless;

Life, short-lived.

I ask you,

Is that a fair bargain?

Should not life live;

And death pass away

Into obscurity?

Conditionally

If death

Is a sleeping,

I shall bid my soul

To wake

At the appointed hour.

And I shall arise,

And go forth,

And meet my new self

In a life's morrow.

Whom shall I be?

Homecoming

Let me go home to die,
No matter where home may be;
Let me return, to vie
With ev'ry memory.

Let me be laid to rest
Under a friendly sky—
If I must pass, at best,
Let me go home to die.

Sleep

Sleep—what is sleep?
Man is endowed
with a few microscopic years
to spend as his conscience directs,
yet at birth he is indebted,
obligated to spend more than half
of those years
> in
> sleep.

And sleep is part payment
on a debt never paid . . .

Balance

The night has its somethings and its nothings.

Try to separate the somethings from the nothings

while the night whitens into day,

> *for soon you will be confronted with*

> > *the day's somethings*

> > *and the day's nothings.*

Distance

If there were no distance,

how dull and stagnant life would be—

for the miles make separations

that blossom into sweet,

heart-quickening returns for the wanderers,

and meetings with memory-faces

that belong in the pages

of the Closed Book . . .

Regret

I asked a couple of migrating birds
   to tell me
if there was something new under the sun
   if we had something to look
   forward to
   besides that maddening horizon
   always a step away
I asked them
   if there was something
   in store for us
   next year
besides the same old tale
   we'd heard for years before
and they told me strange things
   I couldn't understand:

I'm sorry I couldn't pass them on
   to you.

II.

To Be, To See,
To Say

Creation

If the world were wordless
And mine were
The choice
One word
To create
It
Would not be
Money
Nor
Riches
Nor
Even happiness.
No,
None of these.
My word would be
Simple,
All inclusive,
Eternal—
Happiness itself.
For
My word would be
Love.

Obstacles

What if

>your hair does get in your eyes

for one fleeting moment

>and you falter

>or take the wrong turn in the road?

It won't be

>the first time

>or the second,

>the first human

>or the second

it has happened to . . .

There's always time

>to stop and sweep the hair

>from your eyes;

there's always time

>to go back

and take the right turn

>in the road . . .

Idly

To shame, those of us

who in our very weaknesses

propagate idle talk,

knowing idle talk

breeds more than idle

sorrow,

and more than idle sorrow

breeds more than idle

tears.

2

God made the number two
   a half-moon
   and a bar . . .

   A moon
for those deserving it;
   a bar
   shutting out
   the undesirables.

Plantings

Kind words cost nothing,
They are free;
No charge for acting
Affectionately.
The same is true
For tenderness—
It is so easy
To express;
No debt to pay—
You merely say,
"I love you," and
It grows from there;
You simply show
How much you care
In words so plain
They're understood
By heart;
Thus we obtain
The hope we need,
The growing seed
Of love.

First

Most of us have discovered
     predecessors
haunting us at each turn
     someone before—
before in love, in living
     first.
We'd like to be first
     just once—
     only once, Lord
     we'd like to be there
before anyone else—
     let us be first—
     first
     in something
before we pass.

Reminder

Let us not forget that we have purposes,
hopes, plans, ambitions, desires;
let us not forget these—
let us not idly pass them by,
for they are living—
the true life.

Let us not squander
fifty or sixty hop-toad years
existing for mere existence's sake;
let us make each of these years
an acorn for others to plant,
and still others to nurture
and make grow;
we have lives to live—
let us not forget . . .

The Master Quest

There is a courage known to few
   Upon this earth,
The sum of all the highest and the true:
   The noblest worth.

There is an iron spirit daring all—
   It shall not die.
Within the priceless few some higher call
   Must reach the sky.

The constant will, the heart and soul
   Must win the fray;
No higher victory, no greater goal—
   No other way.

Who takes a stand upon the right,
   Who dares the best;
Who keeps the colors highest in the fight—
   That name is blest.

Recognition

To find the best,
      And be it;
To find the work,
      And do it;
To find the need,
      And fill it—
The mark of a finer man.

When people call,
      To answer.
To go beyond
      The dreamer,
To make the dream come true;
      When others quit,
      To linger,
And carry on,
      A fighter—
And thus the legend grows
      Of service to humanity,
Unselfish to the end—
A portrait of a friend.

Song of the Sea
(For Bill, Oct. 20, 1947)

Till the echoes of Taps die out over the blue,

And the spray no more touches my face;

Till the comrades I know bid a last adieu,

And I'm no longer running the race;

While I'm yet at the helm, and the oceans are mine,

And the wind and myself are still free,

O, I'll sail for all ports on the white-capped brine,

For a ship is the home for me, for me,

A ship is the home for me!

III.

Tender Tokens

What Love Is

Love is play, and love is tease,

Love is "thank you," love is "please;"

Love is more of "we" and "us,"

Love is being courteous;

Love's the smile no lie can make,

Love's the look you can't mistake;

Love is patient in all things,

Love's unselfish creditings;

Love is "take me by the hand,"

Love is "hold me, understand;"

Love is silence—words unsaid,

Love is hopes unlimited;

Love is fair, and love is kind,

Love sees all, yet love is blind;

Love is giving, love is share,

Love is showing how you care;

Love's from God, a gift of His . . .

These, and more, are what Love is.

March 20, 1949

They call this the first day of spring,
but I answer:
I know spring of old,
I have known it
many days before this.

They tell me God set this day for spring,
but I say:
spring lives and slumbers in men's hearts,
but to be wakened,
and man himself
makes today spring and yesterday winter.

To the rest I say this:
you gave me spring a moon ago;
you took crying wind and made it laughter;
you took bitter cold
and transformed it into a new warmth,
for I stood by the fireside of your heart
and let spring enter my fingertips
and circulate through me,
long before the calendar
aged itself into this day . . .

October 18, 1952

Across the years a leaf may fall,

a twig may bend;

but over all

the branches tower.

This is the hour

to count the rings;

to see the newborn buds,

and marvel at the song

of wind that sings above

the roots, the girth of it . . .

so strong

our tree of love.

Beauty

Beauty is in liquid movements
of a snow-fresh girl;
the soft outline of graceful
breasts;
Beauty is the sweet yield
of searching lips
and the warm touch of a small
hand;
Beauty is all these, and more—
Beauty is love and love is life
and life is you
and you are Beauty.

Devotion

I'd tramp the roads
to hell and back for you,
      Love,

even
to the ember-ends,
following old trails,
slashing new ones.

Lord! I'd do anything for you,
      Love.
No task too difficult,
no obstacle too high:

no love so great,
      Love.

Bringing

If I could bring you music,
If I could bring you song,
If I could find the words I need
To say that you belong
    Within my heart;
If ever I could tell you,
If ever I could show
How much you mean to all my life,
If ever you could know—
    Where would I start?
I'd need a world of waterfalls,
Of flowers in the spring,
Of lakes and mountains,
Sea and shore,
Of ev'ry beautied thing.
I'd want a quiet moment
Of looking in your eyes
Until the words I covet
Would lovingly arise.

Duration

I shall love you
till the last night and the last sleep
pass over, when I shall be
a stranger to this earth
and my craving for your beauty
is satisfied.

I shall dream of you
in all the spaces of mental quiet,
till the thought of you no more
brings a throbbing to my brain
and your presence
is dissolved by death.

Possession

I got you.
I say you are everything.

I claim your lips
are all that sweetness is;
and I avow
the depths of your eyes to be
my glimpse of what life can hold.

I say
your hands were made
to hold and shape two futures—
your hair to sweep the greatest love
from baffling wind and rain.

I got you.
I say you are me.

I got you.
I say you are everything.

Bestowal

You gave me a wonderful gift today,
    that only you can give,
and I shall keep it always in
    the place where my dreams live;
you gave me a wonderful gift today
    with the innocence of a child;
I had a beautiful gift today . . .
    you smiled.

To a Child
For Kathy

Do you know how much I love you,

Can you feel how much I care?

When I look in your eyes

Do you realize

The wonders I see there?

Such a sweetness and a beauty,

And a love I want to share;

Do you know how much I love you—

Can you feel how much I care?

Memory

Memory of you
is a blood-red poppy,
gently smiling
at an orange sun.

Memory of you
is a handful of comets
showering down
on a stack of love poems
three thousand years written
yet the same
memory
the same lip-red
poppies
the same flashing
comets.

Lost Window

For a lost window to look through
and see a world of other eyes
and other horizons;
for a lost hand and lost lips
and lost kisses taken and given
to be lost by four winds—
God, the lives that are given,
God, the suicides and lost memories
        falling out of lost windows
        dying on lost pavements
        near lost onlookers
        in a lost world . . .

Parting

Parting may be likened
to a thread,
that strand by strand
gives up the ghost
and dies.

IV.

Personations

Anna

Anna had a last name
that sounded like
the official title of the pot of gold
at the end of the elusive rainbow.
Everybody laughed when he heard it
and wondered where she got it
and why didn't she go before the judge
to have it legally changed
so as to spare herself
the torture of the unfamiliar?

Anna remembers that name as being one
respected in the old country—
one affixed to a thousand documents
for the people. Anna couldn't see
wiping that name away with a judge's
handkerchief, like some idle tear
shed but quickly forgotten—
Anna prefers the wry faces
and ridicule—
there are those who must remember.

Carnelli

I used to think Carnelli
didn't have a damn thing
under that battered old hat
of his (you know—the one
with the slits in it
to let in cool air on a
summer's night) but a
half-bald head and a laugh
that made you forget everything,
till one day he suddenly
began spewing forth about
Omar Khayyám and Eddie Poe
like they were old friends of
his, personal-like, and I
leaned back listening, with
mouth partly gaped.

Carnelli is a smart old geezer,
by hell, but how was I to know
when all I saw was a battered hat perched above
a forgetful laugh?

Factory Girl

What?
What's thet in m' hair?
Why
Thet's lint, son.
You cain't 'scape
Lint.

What?
What's thet 'round m' eyes?
Why,
Them's wrinkles an'
Lines, son.
Fact'ry girls
Cain't 'scape
Wrinkles an' lines.

What?
Why am I a-workin' heer?
Gotta make a livin', son—
Gotta make a livin'.

What?
What good's thet kin' a livin'?
Why
I don' know, son.
Reckon
Hit rilly ain't no livin'
Atall.

Earth and Its Master

In his well-worn earth Samuel grubs,

occasionally tossing a defiant gaze

to the rocky mountains

where originated the stones

he stumbles over, the stones

that make his battered plow sing

a mourner's song

over

a red earth wounded, a song

heard above Samuel's curses

flung to a cackling wind . . .

Philosopher

Joe was a philosopher
But then, who wouldn't be,
At twenty a week?
Joe wiped some of the sweat
From his forehead and looked at me.
"Life is a penny, son," he said.
When he saw the look on my face
He assured me,
"Oh, it's got 'two heads,' all right.
Only trouble is, it don't ever land
On the rim. One side's Heaven
And the other's Hell . . .
And you toss the thing ten million times
And maybe it lands one way one time
But t'other the other, till you get
Kinda' tired of throwing the damn thing up,
And you get to not caring which-a-way
The thing lands till one day you throw it
High, and by the time it lands you're done dead . . .

And by grannies you never know while you're alive

Whether or not it landed in Heaven . . . or Hell."

Joe was a philosopher.

Wonder which way his penny landed?

Mamie

Whatever happened to Mamie?
She had the nicest
   eyes.

Lord, the women hated her.
Lord, the men loved her.

Where's her low laughter
slung at you from soft shoulders?

Where are the warm and free kisses,
the love she had to give
and the men who took it?

Whatever happened to Mamie?
She had the nicest
   eyes.

Dirt

"Ain't nothin' like dirt," says the farmer,
plowing between cotton rows in the sun.

"Good old terra firma," says the navy man,
just off a life raft in the Pacific.

"Thank God for soil," says the city gardener,
saving money on the grocery bill.

"There's nothing like good dirt," says the
gravedigger,
throwing in the last small shovelful.

(Here and there it is written: from earth to earth
back and out again, all life is dirt, there's no
such thing as dirty—life is dirt and life is clean so
dirt must be clean.)

Wash Day

Millie scrubs her hands away
on a worn wooden scrub board
close by the black, four-legged pot
over an open corncob fire.
Millie uses soap
made by these same hands
with strong lye and hunks
of melted-down kitchen grease.
As she rubs the red clay dirt
out of Bill's faded overalls,
Millie yearns for a big-city washing machine
and time to spend reading
the latest romance novel
that lies untouched on the kitchen table.

Louise presses a button
and watches indifferently as her husband's
new white shirts
are rotated wildly about
by the latest marvel in washing machinery.

Louise pours a bit of soap

from a brightly colored package

into the top of her machine

and yawns, bored, as she thumbs through

her well-worn copy of the latest

romance novel, dreaming

of a comfortable life

in the green and spacious country

where chickens cluck and scratch idly

in a well-swept front yard . . .

V.

Georgia I Sing

Broom Sedge

I sing of you, broom sedge—
you cover quickly.

I bow to you—
you who blankets

fields, and destroys
man's forgotten furrows.

You make us forget, broom sedge—
the easy forgetters:

you help us on—
Come, cover all . . .

Old Woman

Rock Softly,
Old woman . . .
Dream deeply.

Close your tired eyes.
Let memories
Rise within you . . .
Memories cannot hurt.

Remember,
Old woman.
Dream deeply,
While you
Rock softly . . .

Snow

God whitewashed th' groun' t'day.

He musta' had aigs f' brekfas' this mornin',

'Cause some uh th' salt plumb missed 'iz plate

'N 'tickled ol' terry firmy's back.

Bet 'f I'd been up thar in hevun,

Sharin' m' bakun with th' anjuls,

I'd 'a swore th' ol' globe looked lik'

A whit' fence without a gate,

So's th' peepul couldn't git out.

But th' lazy ol' Earth roz up on its haunches

Lik' a great houn' dawg

'N shuk itself,

'Till all th' purty whit' 'uz gone,

'N th' same ol' shaggy coat showed agin,

A big mess uv cullurs, all wern 'n frazzled.

Seems like' ol' mongrul Earth's 'a standin' hyer

Unsartin lik',

Waitin' f' God t' sen' down a good rain
'N comb 'iz matted beard . . .
Unsatizfied with a k'v'rin uh silv'ry white.

God whitewashed th' groun' t'day,
But a ungrateful world shuk it off.

Conversation with a Pool

In your stored-up, crystalline beauty,

what do you hold for me?

Am I the poet, swimming in your

reflected light—that speck

on the sky's brow? You quiver so.

Is it the wind, or your own foretelling?

The wind knows. Perhaps he moans the answers to you.

Will you not tell me? You and I are brothers,

you know. We are both mirrors, answerers.

Clasp my hand. My brotherhood

has need of you. Quench my thirst

for knowledge, and I shall clear

your surface of Life's impurities, that you

may be a greater mirror.

Granite

This treasured mark of memory,
Raised up in polished symmetry;
This stone beneath the Georgia sod—
A monumental work of God.

To a Georgia Rock

Today, I hold you in my hand;
yet in the dim past
your size would have dwarfed my own.
Who knows—perhaps years long ago
when you were still a part of greater things
you rested on the shore
of what is now Britain, or Alaska, or even China.
Buffeted by ageless winds, ceaseless tides,
you lost that groaning weight
and moved slowly, century by century.
Even by human hands, idly tossing,
your ever-decreasing bulk
was transported.
Now here am I,
holding you within my grasp
as others have held you
in days gone by.
And I marvel at the history you might tell
were you able to speak;
at the story of your own creation;
and the thousand and one things
connected with you
in all your seeming insignificance.

Knowing these things
I feel small within myself—
smaller than you will ever be,
though you disintegrate
into the most minute particle.

My Life Is a Tree

In the falling leaf is seen
The quiet death of a life well spent.
In the falling acorn is seen
The germ of another of Earth's monochildren.
Earth to Earth,
Life to Death . . .

My life is a tree,
and its cycles are mine . . .
Acorn to the Earth, Earth to the tree,
Tree to the leaf, leaf to the Earth.

Arbor Found

I lose myself among the trees
To find my soul in forest green;
For in the still, sweet canopies
The loving hand of God is seen
In ev'ry fixed and falling leaf.
No sadness here, nor human grief.
With branches to the wind unfurled,
The forest trees are God's best world.

Dream Flight

I rose from the floor of the forest
On the wings of a circling bird,
And the breath of the mountains carried
My soul where no murm'ring was heard.

In the stillness below in the forest,
In the shadows and patches of sun,
I could see all I wanted of heaven
On earth where my life had begun;
And I soared on the breath of the mountains
Like the hawk and the eagle and dove,
And I knew from the heights calm and peaceful,
I was safe in the arms of His love.

O to climb up the currents of heaven
With the feathered and freest of flight
As I did in a dream of God's Spirit,
In the hush of a silvery night.

Foreseason

With spring will come the long-awaited birds
To bring their calls and sing their songs in words
That only Nature knows and understands.
The days grow longer and the joy increases,
The soul is stronger in God's warming sun,
And ultimately truth is in the thesis
That love is born where Nature's work is done.

Summer Georgia

Heat rising,
  raining down;
pavements protesting,
  throwing back
  degrees
  unwanted.
I cannot blame you
  for being
  sun.
The worker ball
  must follow its destiny,
  a call to burn,
  task unlimited,
  eon assigned
in flare and flame,
  keeping promises
  unwritten,
  unspoken,
laid down by spirit,
called to glory
  after glory:
days unending, heat
  rising,
  life growing.

Late Summer

The ridges are autumning . . .

red and yellow

daubed onto green

alter

the summer fashion,

for Nature is a lady,

and last season's

apparel

is this season's

dust cloth.

God's Coloring Book

The woolly trees cling tightly to the hills;
Now green, then golden yellow fills
  The Great Palette;
The orange leaf soon red to ruby burns,
As autumn into somber winter turns
  With no regret.

Again the story of the ages told;
As witnesses of time, now we behold
  The passing scene.
In sleep, the ancient season respite shares,
As Nature in her wisdom says her prayers
  For coming green.

Thoughts on Thanksgiving

The fall comes, and tired leaves

Can hold their green no longer.

The magic of Nature imparts to these leaves—

Crowning brief lives with royal splendor—

A scarlet and yellow glory.

Silently they glide on the breath of the ages

Down to Mother Earth,

There to carpet its barren expanses.

And the leaves sing their thanksgiving.

Perhaps this change,

As inevitable as the passing of time,

Effects in the heart of man

The same rejuvenation.

He partakes of the intangible nourishment

Of Mother Earth, breathes the breath of the ages,

And becomes, as the transfigured leaf,

A new being.

And man sings his thanksgivings.

VI.

Up Ridge

Mountain Morning

Fog that hovers over the red earth . . .
you are the morning's breath.

Sun that hovers over the mountains . . .
you are the morning's lantern.

God that hovers over the still world . . .
You are the morning's life.

Mountain Prayer

Fresh footprints

In the newly-plowed earth;

A dark mountain

With moonlight in her hair;

Honeysuckle scents

On the evening air;

Snow patches over the nearby foothills;

Mountain pine

Conversing with the wind—

No need for words

In a mountain prayer.

Mountain Stream
For Yvonne

From these musical waters
Deer have drunk their fill;
Cherokee maidens
Swam here, their laughter
Echoing over the gurgle
of the rapids.
Bronzed warriors
Stalked the wily bear
Along these silent green banks,
Who in turn
Patiently waited
For the brilliant flash
That announced the arrival
Of a mountain trout.
Gold too lured in later years
The prospector's pan,
Before the California fever
Swept all before it.

Today I stand
Where a lonely footlog
Gives proof
Of the white man's encroachment;
And I seem to hear a yearning
Rising up from the rippling waters,

Crying to recall
Those happier days.
But there is no answer;
No rustling sound
Of Georgia deer;
No laughing maidens,
No hunting cries
Or splash of brown paw
In the cool depths;
And gone is the panner's
Cry of discovery.
Nothing
Save these musical waters,
Swiftly moving,
Ever moving
Like the stream of years
Over the sands of time,
Giving voice to its story
Only to those
Who close their present-day eyes
And bend their ears
To a sweeter music
In a sweeter tongue.

Night Sounds in North Georgia

Night sounds in North Georgia . . .
Ever
Heard them?

Katydids swapping lawyer-talk
From one oak to another,
Just proving
You can't win an argument.

Jarflies and crickets
Trying to outdo the katydids.

Bay of a lonesome hound
Somewhere in the distance,
Lending an eerie touch.

Deep bass voice of an ol' bullfrog
Grumbling about things in general.

Cry of a whippoorwill
Touching your very soul . . .
Echoing . . . echoing . . .

All these
Blended into a mountain rhapsody
Lulling you
To sleep.

Song of the Idle Wheel

The water swirls beneath me now,
  but I am still.
O Pioneer—
  once I ground corn for you,
  feeding the hungry mouths,
  my creak and groan
  an old fiddler's tune
  you understood and loved.
You old ones—
  I ask you to remember me
  as I once was.
To you, coldhearted progress,
  I say I was good, I was useful,
  I was great—I ruled
  and was majestic.
Laugh if you must at my rotted timbers,
my tottering supports and rusted iron.
Scorn an old wheel idle in age,
its grave near a broken dam
and a ramshackle shack.

Once I hummed here

a carefree song,

and life was ecstasy,

and I—I was power.

Forget me not now,

though fallen I am

into disgrace, disuse,

unheralded and unsung.

I say once I was great,

once I was useful, had power,

made lives run in tune

with my revolutions.

I say you cannot cast me out,

I say I shall not die.

The water swirls beneath me yet;

unmoving, I will rest.

Cherokee Sunset

(In memory of Walesca, a Cherokee maiden)

Sunset over Pine Log Mountain . . .

I stand before a vast fireside

in restful silence

watching day

melt into night.

In the hush before darkness

long fingers of light

engrave promises

of brighter dawns to come

in gold and multicolored hues.

The compelling music

of the sunset wind

caresses the green pines

just as the last glowing embers

flash brilliantly

and slowly die away . . .

VII.

Asphalt, Concrete, & Steel

Destinations

Everything comes to the city.
    Everything
    comes up from the earth
    to meet concrete and asphalt
all pigeons, all pigeon-beings
    must come to the clamor
    must stoop for crumbs
everything rides the street-bus
    on a well-chartered passage
    to somewhere in the quilted city
everything
    comes to the city
    everything
must go back to the cool moist earth
    after meeting
    hot, dry concrete
    and sticky asphalt.

Equalitarian Pavements

Equalitarian pavements—
they must come to you
they must tread your way
they must come down
> *from the buildings*
> *from the many-windowed*
> *white-collar buildings*
they must come up
> *from the sewers*
> *from the dank, dark sewers—*

> *all gushing forth*
> *from ten thousand*
> *door-mouths—*

Equalitarian pavements—
> *you, the equalizer—*
> *all must come to you . . .*

Redlight

See the light change,
while a mingling changes with it.
And at the moment
life hinges on a red,
green or yellow dot,
suspended in air.
Yet they obey. The light is law.
And years from now
their lives will still be governed
by a colored dot
dangling in the air.

The thinker sees other things
in that light. He sees it as a symbol
of millions of listless beings,
swayed, pushed, shoved, driven
by similar little lights.

And then the thinker
sees the light has changed,
and he obediently crosses the street
with the mingling . . .

Street Singer
(Athens, Georgia, 1947)

The blind man

strums a broken-down guitar

while he sings

a mountain ballad,

listening for the sound of coins

in a battered tin cup.

And there is a faraway look

in the once-were eyes.

The dark and hollowed sockets

are harbors for thoughts . . .

thoughts

of what might have been . . .

Sidewalk

Sidewalk,

I see furrows in your brow,

and are those crow's feet

at your eyes

blending with the care-lines

of your cheeks

and the humor-traces

at your mouth?

Yes, on your timeworn face

have trod

how many millions of feet?

How many?

How many happy feet?

Or sad? Weary?

Light or heavy?

Ah, here is where

young girls have stood

breathlessly, to be kissed

by lovers,

and here is the place
where babies have toddled,
uncertain, light of foot,
to grow and tread
this way again and again,
to plant their cares
in this cement,
to have them grow
as they have grown
out of the small beginnings.

Sidewalk,
I see furrows in your brow,
and many stories
on your silent tongue.

Trash

Bet you have a story to tell, trash . . .

two theater tickets, half torn,

these the smiling eyes,

the clinging hands;

jagged envelopes and black-stained stamps,

someone had a letter from God,

someone loves again, lives again . . .

ah, you memories

wrapped in old newspapers

and trash, littering

so many city streets . . .

Under a Street Lamp

Cheap lips
Cheap smiles
Cheap laughter . . .
Cheap love.

Street by Moonlight

The street holds hands with fingers of moonlight.
Let them love. Theirs is a love story . . .

A lonely cat sits in a lonely doorway
and looks at a lonely sky.
The moon has a lost meaning to him.
He has two moon-eyes—
the white blurb above, but one.

There walks a man, alone.
He and the moon and the cat are brothers—
of separate races, yet brothers
in the same light.

Voice the moon and the street.
Give them lips to speak.
Hear the story of a cat in a lonely
doorway, moonfingers, and a man alone,
for this is a love story,
and only love stories merit telling.

Rails in the Morning

Somewhere along the line, whistles wail.
Drowsy dawn rises up on its haunches,
yawning.

Two shining parallels ride the earth's back . . .
on, on together and side by side
is their story.

A paper peddler puts his ear to the wet steel
to hear a distant chug-a-lug.

Somewhere along the line, whistles wail.
Iron monsters ready themselves
for today's mail
and today's hurriers . . .

Good-bye, Streetcars

Good-bye to you, streetcars—
I flick my hand and wave
a cheery good-bye,
yet sadly I wave . . .

    good-bye
to your rhythmical sway
and electric smells;
    good-bye
to your lurch and the laughing
grind of metal upon metal;
    au revoir
to the worn leather straps;
good-bye to all these . . .

    farewell
to the shining metal rails
crisscrossing here and there—
we shall miss you—
we shall look for your trails . . .

good-bye
to the rustic conductors
and the familiar sight
of the sweeping curve of your roof,
the hiss of your brakes . . .

good-bye, streetcars,
we shall miss you—
good-bye.

VIII.
Still Small Voice

God Give Me Words

God give me words,
For only they are living;
Mortality
Is born and dead;
In the same breath
And there is no return;
But a word,
A purposeful word,
Has no death—
Only
The conception
(And words
May be conceived,
Though they may be born before)
And the afterlife;
No intermediate
Period
With wonderings
Of the before and after,
Not even the
Being.
God give me words,
For words were,
And are,
And shall be.

To Be

With kindness keep

The deepest Love for others.

Love covers all—

The inner, the outer;

No doubter

Long

Resists the strong

And changing power

Of human caring.

Be therefore daring.

Be Love, Be Love, Be Love.

Love Prayer

May your love be

Simple, direct,

In giving or receiving;

Unwavering in intensity,

Unconquerable in adversity.

May you love continually,

Even as you would be loved,

Knowing love is never lost

    When given—

Love lives eternally.

Thanks

Lord, I believe I thank You most

for music—most of all

for stirring music

and millions of crescendos

to uplift, and softer strains

to soothe . . .

Lord, You must have made music

just for me . . .

Place in the Sun

Lord, we ask of You
a place in the sun,
one small recompense
for having lived and died
under it,
where we
may shine upon other fleas
of a shaggy-hound world,
warming hearts
with a bit of hope
and only enough strength
to last through the Darkness
until the Dawning . . .

Harmony

Where the Sower and the Reaper
Are joined together,
The Inner Jury
Says yes to Life.

In the tally of the fields
Thus one accord
Symphonizes their yields;
By day and night
The heightened mind
Will gain the Light.

The Lord Is Coming—Make the Way

The Lord is coming—make the way;

behold, salvation cometh;

Our God appears on earth to reign

as ancients have foretold.

His name shall be Emmanuel,

God with us through the ages;

The Promised One, the only Son,

the shepherd of the fold.

The Lord thy God will raise to earth

a prophet of thy children,

And He shall feed them, He shall be

their shepherd in the night.

And this His name: He shall be called

the Lord of Righteousness,

Exalted One, the chosen Son,

and our eternal light.

Desire of ev'ry nation come,
and fill the world with glory;
Teach us Thy ways and bring to pass
Thy judgment on the earth.
O Mighty God, O Christ the Lord,
our Savior and Redeemer,
Come highest Son, come Holy One,
the world awaits Thy birth.

Behold, He sends His Messenger,
the promised Prince of Peace,
The Voice of Heaven, Lamb of God,
the true Messiah, King!
His great dominion shall not pass,
the Lord of Lords forever;
Thy will be done from sun to sun;
Thine Alleluias ring!

Song of the Wise Men

God in His wisdom sent a star
That we, His servants from afar,
Might see the light, might find the way,
To where the newborn Savior lay.

Yet thought we then a King we'd find
To rule the world and all mankind;
A noble babe of royal birth
Exalted far above the earth.

The Lord Himself gave us a sign
And sealed the vision: David's line
Would raise a King of Israel,
The prophesied Emmanuel.

So come we now with gifts and gold
To witness as it was foretold:
Thou Bethlehem, O lowly one,
Shall bring Him forth—the Holy Son!

A Child, the Christ, Is Born for Us

A child, the Christ, is born for us!
Sing praise! Sing praise!
The Son of God, this morn for us!
Sing praise! Sing praise!

Peace on earth, goodwill to men,
Christ is born to save us!
Blest are we, and blest again
By the Son He gave us.

> *Born to save us, born to save us;*
> *Praise and glory! Born to save!*

From Bethlehem a shining star!
Sing praise! Sing praise!
Low shepherds and high kings afar
Sing praise! Sing praise!

Gather up the world and sing,
Christ is born to love us;
Now a Savior, now a King,
Come to reign above us!

> *Born to love us, born to love us;*
> *Praise and glory! Born to love!*

Lullaby, Holy Child

Lullaby, Holy Child,
Now the world rejoices!
See the glory all about?
Hear the angel voices?
    See the star, how it shines,
    Lighting all around You!
    Kings and shepherds come as one—
    By His sign they found You.

Baby Lord, Baby Lord,
Lying in a stable; will they love You, will they care,
Will the world be able?
    Little Christ, Little Christ,
    Sleeping in a manger;
    Will they hear You, will they know,
    Will You be a stranger?

Blessed One, Blessed One,
Born to adoration;
Gift of Heaven, Son of God,
King of ev'ry nation;
    Son of Love, Son of Love,
    Can You bear the glory?
    When it's over, when it's done,
    Will they know Your story?

They Crucified Him

They crucified Him! Where is He,
   The gentle one of Galilee?
What news is there—what seen or heard—
   Has Jesus yet fulfilled the Word?

The news is good! He is not dead!
   The cross is conquered where He bled!
He is the Christ, the Blessed One,
   The Lamb of God, the proven Son!

Look you no more, He is not there,
   His pow'r revealed—the tomb is bare!
Now risen He, and seen of men—
   Doubt you no more! He lives again!

Why Hast Thou Forsaken Me?

Why hast Thou forsaken me,

Laid my body on a tree?

Now afflicted, now oppressed,

Weight of ages on my breast,

Now despised, rejected, lone,

Am I not Thy Son, Thine own?

Is it nothing, passing by?

Crowned and wounded, it is I!

Where is now the shouting throng,

Gift of palm, and praising song?

Need I die the lowest way,

All iniquity to pay?

God, my God, I thirst, I die;

Was I born to crucify?

Father, must I bear the shame,

for redemption in my name?

God, they know not what they do;

Is it finished, is it through?

O my Father, let me see
Why Thou hast forsaken me;
Dark the moment, dark the trial
Of the cross, a bitter vial.
Stripe and sorrow, nail and thorn,
Thine the glory in their scorn!

Look upon humanity
Waiting for a sign from me;
God forgive! I trust, obey;
Thine the answer, Thine the way;
Let Thy will be done, as I
Bear my cross, and gladly die.

May Jesus Christ Be Born Again

May Jesus Christ be born again today;
A stable, and a star to show the way;
With shepherds on a hill,
When all the night is still,
And kings to find where child and mother stay.
A time of wonder once again is here—
The Son is come, with hope and joy and cheer.
With song and glorious Light,
Come angels in the night—
May Jesus Christ be born again this year.

Let Jesus Christ be born again for you;
In ev'ry one, bring love and joy anew;
The sound of angel song,
In praise the whole night long,
When once again the child of God is due.
Now wise men bring their gifts to prove his worth,
As Jesus comes to hearts upon the earth;
We tell the story old,
The greatest story told—
The ageless miracle, His holy birth.

Road Desired

May I be a simple soul,

Love for others be my goal,

Giving more than I would gain,

Helping those in need or pain;

Being one who, like the Son,

Takes the cross and carries on,

And, whatever road I meet,

End my journey at His feet.

Dear Lord, I Give Myself to Thee

Dear Lord, I give myself to Thee
To do with as Thou wilt;
O Christ, Thou art new life for me,
Redeemed of ev'ry guilt.
My strong support and comfort be,
My friend above all friends;
Abide with me O blessed Lord
Till all my doubting ends.

Dear Lord, my faith looks up to Thee
In all my earthly needs;
Amazing grace that sets me free
And all my hunger feeds.
Cleanse me O Lord of ev'ry doubt,
Of hopelessness and fear;
Forgive my weak unsure belief
And keep Thy presence near.

Dear Lord, I pray Thy will to see,
Thy way to understand;
To find my highest goal in Thee—
To follow Thy command.
Bring me Thy gentle peace, until
Thine ev'ry thought I know;
That through Thy grace, and by Thy pow'r,
My cup shall overflow.

Dear Lord, I speak Thy name and hear
Sweet answer to my pray'r;
A hope that overcomes all fear
And cancels ev'ry care.
Now kneeling at Thy cross, O Lord,
I feel Thy hand in mine;
Thy love is calling to my soul—
My heart is wholly Thine.

Rx: the Great Physician

Lord, I've not had my dose of smiles today . . .
I'll take mine now.

Last time You forgot my drop of fearlessness.
But I know You've been busy . . .
Send mine down soon.

And Lord, when You make my prescription up
Please don't fail to send
My spoonful of understanding . . .
I need it badly now.

And oh yes, Lord, we can't exclude
An extra large dose of hope . . .
I spilled mine yesterday.

And You might add an ounce of love
And flavor the whole
With faith and belief . . .
My supply is getting low.

Lord, I've not had my dose of these today . . .
I'll take mine now.

Take Me, Lord

Take me, Lord, and make me, Lord,
A child of Thine;
Take my cup, Lord, fill it up
With holy wine;
Touch me, Lord, that I may be
A loving soul;
Touch my heart, Lord—ev'ry part—till
I am whole.

Feed me, Lord, I need Thee, Lord—
My daily bread;
On my journey, light the path
Where I am led;
And I pray, Lord, if I stray, Lord,
Understand;
Lead me, guide me, stay beside me,
Take my hand.

Tell me, Lord, what I must do
To follow Thee;
Let Thy will be done this day;
Lord, walk with me;
Keep me safe, and when life's done,
Then, by Thy word—
Coming softly, coming gently,
Take me, Lord.

Acceptance

God's love comes in from forever,

And goes to the end of mind;

Love illumines the day

As it travels the way

From Spirit to all humankind.

We draw from an infinite caring,

As much as our hearts receive;

And the love we use

Is the love we choose

From the depths of the love we believe.

Comfort

There is no way to turn the tide of sorrow
Until the waves have washed upon the shore—
Until the ebb of day becomes tomorrow.
And yet the highest mark can be no more
   Than day can hold.

There is no grief the greater than the hour;
No shadow comes unless the light appears.
There is no longing larger than the power
Of God to fill our hearts and make our tears
   Just one day old.

Prayer One

Cover me

With Your Spirit,

O God:

Use my heart

For Your glory,

Tongue for

Your Word

Hands for

Your giving.

Place me

In the midst

Of need;

Help me feed

The hungry

Of mind

Or spirit

Or body.

Let me
Shine Your
Everlasting light
On life,
And make it
Good, kind,
And loving . . .
Thus, serving.

Giving to God

Giving to God is very like
His giving of love to me;
A special way to show I bow
In thanks for all I see.

Thus in the garden of my soul,
I plant the seeds of care
That grow into the greater good
For all mankind to share.

So let me part, and cheerfully,
With that which I've been given,
Well knowing that a thankful heart
Is ever near to heaven.

Listening

Sometimes the only one who is not heard
Is God;
Those earthly noises with their long denials
Of human nature's true allegiance
Will not allow that still, small voice
A place in time.
When will we learn such simple truth:
That we must move ourselves closer,
Willing to be His children again?
We give to God a place remote
Until our needs cry out:
"Where is He, why has He forsaken me
Now that I need Him?"
And in our fevered fear we plead,
"O hear us Lord, and if Thou wilt
We never more shall stray from Thee."
The lesson is the answer,
For He was here, and there, and everywhere;
It is ourselves
Who were lost.

Lord, Warm Our Hearts

Lord, warm our hearts as Thou hast touched
The hearts of saints before;
Bring to us all such peace and joy
That we may trust Thee more.
For we who may be lesser than
the souls of early day,
Still need the solace of Thy love
To help us find the way.

Awake within us all the need
To be about Thy will,
That when Thy voice is o'er the land,
Our spirits may be still.
Show us the treasures of Thy word
That tower over time,
Unchanging as the seasons in
Thine own eternal clime.

O what a work Thou hast begun

With such a faithful few,

Those loyal ones who walked the earth

From when the faith was new;

Now choose us, Lord, for service high,

Upon a cause divine,

And like a shepherd, lead us, Lord—

O may our will be Thine.

How Can We Thank Thee?

For this day our daily bread,
For Thy good, unlimited;
Beauty of the earth and sky,
Oceans wide and mountains high,
Light of morning, stars of night,
Cold of autumn, winter white—
How can we thank Thee,
How can we thank Thee?

For the sun that shines by day,
Fixed with love to light our way;
For majestic trees of green
In the quiet forest seen;
Birds and flowers Thou hast made,
All creation here displayed—
How can we thank Thee,
How can we thank Thee?

For the living of this day,

For Thy Son to show the way,

For Thy blessings big and small,

For the love that's given all;

For the joy that now we share

In Thy everlasting care—

How can we thank Thee,

How can we ever thank Thee?

I See Him

I see Him in a mother's smile,
A child at play;
I see Him when the sun comes up
At break of day;
I see Him in a loving pray'r,
A bluebird's wings;
I see Him in a single rose—
The little things.

I see Him in a sky of blue
And in the rain;
I see Him in the greatest joy
And deepest pain;
I see Him in a baby's cry—
Each time He's there;
His hand is in the rainbow's end—
He's ev'rywhere.

He's with me when the days begin,

And when they're o'er;

I see Him in a thousand ways

And still there's more;

And when at last my time is past

And life grows dim;

I'll know the peace, the sweet release

When I see Him.